Joscha Remus
Berlin – City Guide for Children

D0900713

Joscha Remus

BERLIN

City Guide for Children

Illustrated by Sibylle Vogel,
translated by Robert Scott McInnes

Picus Verlag Wien

This City Guide for Children is also available in German

Berlin – Stadtführer für Kinder,

by Joscha Remus and Sibylle Vogel

ISBN 978-3-85452-145-7

Copyright © 2010 Picus Verlag Ges.m.b.H, Wien
Alle Rechte vorbehalten
Grafische Gestaltung: Dorothea Löcker, Wien
Druck und Verarbeitung:
Druckerei Theiss GmbH, St. Stefan im Lavanttal
ISBN 978-3-85452-155-6

www.picus.at

Contents

The following symbols will make it easier for you to find your way in this book:

 5   More information in Tour 5.

   Houses described in a tour.

   The route you should take.

   Start of a tour. At the beginning of each tour, you will find a list of the public transport to take you to the starting point.

   Tips for special tours for children, or more information in the introduction or chapter »Other Things to See and Do in and around Berlin«.

Here, you can make a drawing or fill in something.

This means that you should take a close look or solve a puzzle. You will find the solutions at the back of the book.

How to use this book

Before you set out on your journey to discover Berlin, here are a few tips about how to make the most of this book.

First of all, you will learn how Berlin started out as two small villages that developed into a big city and how the people used to live in Berlin. You will be amazed to find out all the things a swamp can be turned into and the career a little fisherman's island can make over the centuries.

Then you can set out on a series of tours to discover the city by yourself. You don't need much equipment; maybe a pencil, sharp eyes and some imagination. We have selected the tours so that you will spend a lot of time in pedestrian precincts, in squares and in green areas.

Of course, there are many more things to see and do in a city like Berlin than can be included in our book. Some people even say that a lifetime would be too short to see all that Berlin has to offer.

That is why we have included a small selection of other destinations that could possibly interest you in chapter 7.

By the way: You will never be really alone in this big city. Two especially experienced guides will accompany you on your tours to explore Berlin: These two children – and a bear – will discover the city along with you. We are sure you will have a lot of fun!

A Brief History of the City

Berlin

Cölln

Ice-age glaciers, swamps ...

Berlin is a very young city – one of the youngest in Europe. Eight hundred years ago, when cities like London, Paris, Rome or Vienna had been in existence for ages, the place where Berlin now lies was mainly swampland, with raging rivers and enormous lakes. Many of the first settlements were located in the middle of a valley that had been formed by melting water from gigantic glaciers – the so-called Urstromtal (Primeval River Valley).

... and the Fishermen's Island

That makes it not at all surprising that fishermen were particularly keen to settle in an area with so much water. This happened in the southern part of today's Spree Island that is also called the Fishermen's Island. It is a pity that the old fishing district to the south of Gertraudenstraße no longer exists. And, the swamplands in the north were drained many years ago and have disappeared. Today, this is the site of the most beautiful museums in the city (see R 3).

They're twins!

Berlin began its career as a city on two small islands in the middle of the wild twists and turns of the River Spree. This is where the sister cities of Cölln and Alt-Berlin were founded opposite each other. There was a ford – a shallow place in the water – where you could easily cross the river from one city island to the other. Later, bridges were built and the two little towns grew even closer together. In 1307, the citizens of the twin cities built a common town hall.

A town hall over the water

Two of Berlin's oldest bridges in the "Mitte" district bring back memories of this time. Both were made of wood and it is even said that the Berlin-Cölln town hall once stood on the Town Hall Bridge! But, we are sure that the Mühlendammbrücke (Mill Wall Bridge) got its name from the six water mills that used to be located there.

Berlin gets its way

Old Berlin was about twice the size of Cölln and this gave

it a head start when a name had to be chosen for the city. Linguists say that Berlin comes from the Slavonic word for "place in the swamp". That makes sense because we know just how swampy and marshy things were in the Urstromtal.

However, nature experts think that there is a connection between Berlin and the German word for little bear "Bärlein" because, in years gone by, bears used to hunt for fish in the shallows of the Spree between the twin cities. The quarrel over whether the city got its name from the swamps or a little bear have continued to today. All the same – Berlin still sounds a bit like "bear". And it's a lot of fun to say or write Bärlin – the "Bearliners" really like to do it!

In the right column you can see the Old-Berlin city seal from 1280. It shows the Brandenburg eagle and two bears in coats of mail. The bears symbolize the robber barons of the time and the eagle stands for the margrave, the former ruler of Berlin, who protected the town against their attacks.

Margraves, robber barons and funny names – Berlin in the Middle Ages

In the 13th century, Berlin-Cölln became increasingly important as a trading centre. At the beginning, the young twin city only had 4200 inhabitants but the small community soon became wealthy and

powerful. Many Berlin traders mastered the art of carrying out business with faraway cities and countries. They journeyed as far as Russia to get their hands on precious furs. Rye, beer and oak wood from Brandenburg were delivered to Hamburg and Holland and the traders brought spices and Flemish fabrics with them back to Berlin.

A successful deposit

The up-and-coming city lay exactly at the crossroads of old trade routes. The taxes the margraves imposed on the traders rapidly filled their treasure chests. They were so happy about this that they granted Berlin-Cölln many special privileges.

One of these was exemption from duties. Fees were no longer charged for many goods at the city limits. Two other privileges were the so-called rights to "stack" and "deposit". This might sound a bit strange but it proved to be very useful for the Berliners. It forced foreign merchants to offer their wares on the city's markets and – in those days – that was called stacking and depositing. This meant that early on the Berliners were able to buy things at a good price. And, this kind of deposit usually made a profit for the traders from far away.

By the way, the German word for "con man" – Hochstapler, which literally means "high stacker" – comes from this time. In the jargon of the wayfarers and outlaws in those days, it stood for a beggar who pretended to be an elegant gentleman.

Markets, churches and strict rules

The first markets in Berlin were set up near bridges and churches. The Molkenmarkt (Milk Market) can still be found near the Nikolai Quarter in Berlin-Mitte. Even today, it is called a market but dairy products are no longer sold there. In former times, the Cölln fish market was located on the Spree Island alongside the St. Petri Church. Unfortunately, both have now disappeared. And, if they still existed, they would probably be completely hidden by the high-rise buildings. But, Berlin's oldest church remains standing: The Nikolai Church was built of fieldstones between 1220 and 1230. It is located in the centre of a modern district between Spandauerstraße and Rathausstraße right next to the Spree. Today, the church is a museum and concerts are also held there.

Around 1400, Berlin and Cölln already had about 8500 inhabitants and there were more than 1000 houses in the town. The Marien District, as well as the entire historic heart of the city on the Spree Island and the Nikolai Quarter, was run through with many small streets. For a long time, there was not only the water and swampland but also two big

dunes. It was really cramped in the little town of Berlin-Cölln in those days. Most of the people living on the Spree Island were fishermen, and the traders and craftsmen settled on the right bank. Some of the street names in Berlin still recall these mediaeval trades. You will possibly come across the *Leineweber* (Linen Weaver) *Böttcher* (Cooper) and *Hufschmied* (Blacksmith) Streets.

Sausage court

In those days, there were strict rules for everything. The executioners and hangmen were only allowed to live on the outskirts of town near the city walls. For reasons of hygiene, the city's slaughterhouse – called the Wursthof or "Sausage Court" – was set up right next to the water. Dress regulations stipulated that the citizens had to wear plain jackets and coats. There were decrees against pompous, extravagant festivities and games of chance. And – after the last stroke of the clock – no more dancing was permitted on the streets.

Watery beer

In those days, the work the normal people had to do was really strenuous and the food they ate

nowhere near as diversified as it is today.

In the Middle Ages, the Berliners' meals consisted mainly of fish, grain soup, fruit, mushrooms, root vegetables and thin, watered down beer. Life was also very dangerous. Berlin-Cölln never had a real fortress! The Berliners were only protected from being attacked by robber barons and other enemies by a vigilante group as well as a city wall and five massive city gates.

JWD!

That is why they were keen on forming alliances with nearby fortified towns. At the time, the Berliners thought that these towns like Spandau and Köpenick were located "j.w.d" – in the Berlin dialect that means "janz weit draußen" or way out there. It took more than two hours to reach them in a horse-drawn carriage. Today, Spandau and Köpenick are districts of Berlin and only a thirty-minute train ride from the centre of town.

You can find the remains of the medieval city wall built of fieldstones along Waisenstraße.

The great fire

However, a city wall was of no use for fighting against enemies that were hard to beat. In the Middle Ages, the city was struck by the plague many times. But the fire that blazed through Berlin and burned almost the whole city and all the churches and houses in it to ashes in 1380 was much worse than the plague. Thousands of people perished. A knight turned out to be the person who had set fire to the town and was executed. The compassionate ruler exempted the ruined citizens from all taxes for three years.

Like a patchwork rug

In the Middle Ages, Berlin grew bigger and bigger – just like a huge patchwork rug. Over time, new communities were integrated into the city. These included the old settlements of the Templar Order: Mariendorf, Marienfelde and Tempelhof. At the time, Berlin was a citizens' city where the inhabitants were independent and had the final say in all matters. The ancestral seats of the margraves and prince electors were usually located far away in Saxony, Franconia or Luxembourg.

Too many Ottos

Many of these rulers had funny nicknames: There was an Albrecht the Bear and even Friedrich the Fat. And there were a lot of Ottos: Otto the Lazy, Otto the Tall, and Otto the Pious. There was also an Ascanian Prince Otto with the Arrow. He was given that name because he went around for more than a year with an arrow he had been hit by stuck in his head. The end of the citizens' city came with the Hohenzollern Prince Friedrich the Second who was nicknamed Iron Tooth. He was the first to have a castle erected in the city but it looked more like it had been built to ward off an enemy siege. In 1451, this made Berlin a royal seat for the first time in its history. (You will find out more about the castle on one of the tours, see R 3.)

 You can take a journey in time back to the Middle Ages and see how the people lived then at the Düppel Museum Village.

Berlin is bursting at the seams

Around 1550, Berlin had more than 12,000 inhabitants and it had become much too crowded inside the city walls.

The expansion of the castle on the Spree Island had caused more and more people from the surrounding districts to flood into the city. There was a great demand for bricklayers, gardeners and stonemasons at the time because many other residential buildings, bridges, fountains and gardens were being built. The prince elector's residence soon turned into a gigantic building site. Two- and three-storey buildings in the baroque style replaced the small half-timbered houses with their straw or shingle roofs. The Middle Ages disappeared in a hurry in Berlin!

The sinking tower

There was a lot of building going on. But the swampy, muddy subsoil created headaches for even the best architects. The castle building director received the commission to increase the height of a water tower but the pressure caused the soft ground to give way. The 60-metre-high tower sunk down into the depths and the builder fell from favour. The toppled water tower was also used as the treasury and so Berlin had to do without the mint that was located high up in the tower for a while.

The prince electors' residential city becomes a regal capital

The age of the prince electors came to an end in 1701, when Berlin became the capital of the Kingdom of Prussia. King Friedrich I had castles and magnificent gardens built outside the city gates in his attempts to follow in the footsteps of the France's Sun King and his court. There was a lot of dancing and many festivities in Berlin in those days. If you want to see how the kings lived then, have a look at Charlottenburg Castle. It has everything a real castle should have: glittering halls of mirrors, plush baroque furniture, gigantic paintings, long corridors, precious porcelain vases and an enormous garden. Of course, the city was not so magnificent everywhere. Many streets were now lit by lanterns at night but the lanes

14

and courtyards still reeked of garbage and the foul-smelling deposits people left behind them – just like in the Middle Ages. Not all Berliners could afford to have their garbage removed. Poverty had entered the city along with prosperity and there were more and more poorhouses.

Berlin had them to thank for their first silk stockings and, all of a sudden, the restaurants started serving delicate French vegetables like cauliflower and asparagus. The Huguenots were very tolerant and their new ideas influenced intellectual life. Around 1700, every seventh Berliner was French.

The French city

Some of the buildings, parks and castles in Berlin – such as the Charité Hospital, Bellevue Castle or Monbijou Park – still have French names and quite a few Berlin slang expressions still preserve their French origins. A real Berliner calls a meatball a "Bulette" and if he eats it with his hands he says "from the Lamäng" – in French, that is written *á la main.*

Cauliflower and asparagus arrive

The French Huguenots were among the most popular settlers in the new capital. Although they had come to Berlin as poor Protestant refugees in the prince electors' times, many of them soon lived close to the regal court. The Huguenots were wooed by the rulers because they were skilful craftsmen and brought good manners to Berlin. The ladies in

Sedan chairs and hackney cabs

At the beginning of the 18th century, the fine ladies and gentlemen paraded through the gardens in their exquisite clothes and riders trotted along the park avenues on their horses. The first public transportation in Berlin was provided by Huguenot sedan-chair carriers who made it possible for well-off citizens to float through the city on luxuriously padded chairs.

Two-horse fiacres and single-horse hackney cabs bounced along the plastered main streets. The trampling of the horses' hooves became louder and louder and there were many accidents; this forced the king to set Berlin's first speed limit. Horses were forbidden to gallop.

An end to dancing and music

The next king, who was also known as the "Soldier King", made even more things illegal. Friedrich Wilhelm was not at all interested in dancing, singing and making music. In addition, he did not like celebrations, the arts and the theatre. The court painters and musicians were fired

and the opera houses and theatres closed down. He even had the trees in the Lustgarten (Pleasure Garden) chopped down and the flowers pulled out, and turned it into a parade ground. The only things the king really liked were his soldiers. And, he was particularly fond of the well-built men in the Royal Guard who had to be at least 1.88 metres (6'2") tall. Friedrich Wilhelm was also very thrifty and practical. He encouraged all the Berliners to drink a lot of beer so that they would not have to buy the even more expensive tea from Asia. (You can find out more about the Lustgarten on the R 3 tour.)

Old Fritz

Everything changed under his son Friedrich the Great who was later

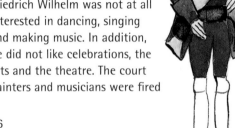

affectionately called "Old Fritz". He really loved music, played the flute and even composed. He whetted the Berliners' appetite for a new vegetable called the potato, abolished torture and distributed free mulberry tree seeds and tiny silkworm eggs among the Berliners. This made it possible for each of the citizens to produce a bit of silk for themselves, provided they had their own garden.

1.90 m.

Although Old Fritz had to go to war a few times, Berlin experienced a heyday of science and the arts during his reign. The  architecture became really impressive and very playful, as can be seen on the facades of the Crown Prince's Palace and State Opera. The old city walls had already been torn down and replaced by a tariff wall much further away to make room for the new settlers. Berlin had as many as 14 city gates and some of them – such as the Brandenburg Gate, Halle Gate and Silesian Gate – are still well known today. (You can find out more about the Brandenburg Gate on the **R 2** tour.)

The man with the column

In 1806, a famous Frenchman – who we know so well because he always liked to keep one hand hidden under a lapel of his coat – rode through the most westerly of these gates with his army. Napoleon Bonaparte's troops occupied the city for two years.

A few years after the French soldiers had looked around Berlin, a Berliner did the same thing in Paris. And, he came up with a good idea.

Ernst Litfass really liked the way the Parisians hung their posters so neatly at certain specific places. It was completely different in Berlin. Here, every businessman, every inventor and every theatre always had something new to advertise and the walls everywhere where completely covered up with posters. This uncontrolled jumble of advertisements only came to an end when Mr. Litfass set up columns throughout the city. They became the only place where the theatres, circuses and soap makers were allowed to display their announcements.

17

The Kremsers

A lot of other innovations were introduced along with Mr. Litfass' columns in the 19th century. Instead of the Huguenot sedan-chair carriers, horse omnibuses made their way through the city. That is what they were really called once, but later the Berliners changed this to Kremsers. Today, the Kremsers are still in use; mainly on Father's Day when up to ten merry men travel through the city in a decorated wagon drawn by two horses. In former times, a trip in a Kremser could have taken you from the Tiergarten (animal reserve) to the Zoo. Today, the word Tiergarten also means zoo in German; but, in the times of the prince electors, it was a hunting ground with deer and wild boar. However, in 1844, real animals began running around in the Berlin Zoo – the first in Germany. Even very exotic ones like peacocks, llamas and water buffalo. (In tours R 4 and R 5., you will find out why they were the first animals in the Berlin Zoo and what they have to do with the Peacock Island.)

The father of all gymnasts

Although the Berliners were very happy with many inventions, such as the new gas lanterns in the streets, the first steam locomotive in Europe and the pretty little garden plots, the Prussian kings at first could not acquire a taste for one of the novelties – and that was gymnastics.

Gymnastics also had to be invented. This was done by a Berliner named Ludwig Jahn. But the rulers, with their Prussian meticulousness, found the wriggles and contortions Jahn – who is still known as the father of gymnastics – performed in the Hasenheide Park not at all to their liking and downright suspicious. That did not even change when flocks of Berliners started doing knee-bends and press-ups in public in the city parks. The people living in the city's palaces could just not imagine anything as ridiculous as sport. And so, public gymnastics were simply forbidden. But many Berliners kept on exercising at home.

18

The imperial city

In those days, there had to be regulations for everything in Prussia – and this was especially true in Berlin. Things had to be where they belonged and that also applied to people. In the so-called Gründerzeit after 1870, the poor people lived in the back courtyards of tenement buildings in what the Berliners still call the "Souterrain" – another French word. The souterrain is located between the ground floor and cellar, half way below street level. You can still find some of these dark apartments in the Kreuzberg, Mitte or Prenzlauer Berg districts. They can be recognized by their narrow, steep

staircases and the tiny windows placed directly on the level of the pavement.

The well-to-do Berliners lived above the souterrain on the Beletage. French again! It literally means "beautiful floor". While the domestic servants, coal dealers and shoemakers sat in their dingy rooms, a little higher up the light flooded into the spacious beletage apartments through large windows. They were sumptuously decorated with stucco, had balconies and their facades were adorned with columns, figures and ornaments.

Full steam ahead!

Everything became even more ordered after a war against the French who had formerly been so admired. Now Berlin had an emperor. An extremely well-ordered one. And, if we want to be as exact as the Prussians, we must add that

there were even three emperors in the year 1888. The last of them, Emperor Wilhelm II, twisted the ends of his moustache sharply upwards with the utmost precision. This was a sign that things were on the rise. His favourite motto was "Full steam ahead!" and Berlin was really moving! New factories and halls were being built all over town where the people toiled away to produce all kinds of goods.

Flying machines and kangaroos

The Berliners were very inventive and liked to try out new things. The engineer Otto Lilienthal made his first attempts at flying, the first public film show in the world took place in a pub called the Prater – the same name as the famous Prater amusement park in Vienna. This is where boxing matches between men and kangaroos were held. The people in Berlin developed a liking for beer with raspberry or

woodruff syrup and the first underground railway came into operation between the Warschauer Straße and Zoo stops. For a long time, it was considered the world's most punctual underground.

In those days, everything was carried out with Prussian briskness and precision. Life in Berlin was usually a very serious matter but that changed radically when a little man from Köpenick showed the Berliners and their nitpicking authorities that it was also possible to laugh at yourself.

The strange captain

The shoemaker Friedrich Wilhelm Voigt bought himself the uniform of a Prussian army captain along with the matching military cap and good shoes in a second-hand shop.

Being dressed up this way and the snappy tone of his voice made him absolutely convincing. The phony captain made his way to the Köpenick town hall with a few soldiers where he simply arrested the mayor and had 4000 marks handed over to him from the city's treasurer's office. Everybody followed his orders as they should. It is said that not only the Berliners but also the Emperor laughed about this successful prank. After a short time in prison, the "Captain from Köpenick" became a famous Berlin figure; a book was written about him, a film made and he even became famous in faraway America.

You can see a memorial to the "Captain from Köpenick" in his complete bogus uniform in front to the town hall in Köpenick. It is located on Rosenstraße at the corner of Alt Köpenick.

The German Republic

Things only started to cheer up in Berlin after the First World War. The Emperor abdicated and the German Republic was proclaimed. Now elected representatives took care of the citizens' wishes. Berlin was able to take

a deep breath and have some fun before absolutely terrible things happened.

The golden years

By the golden 1920s, the quick-witted, cheeky Berlin slang of the common people had long become famous in the theatres. People sang popular Berlin tunes that everybody knew and, from time to time, they liked making fun of others. However a Berliner could become rather touchy if he felt that he was being made to look silly and could say "You have never stuck a candy on a naked man's shirt yourself" meaning that you should go and pull your own leg.

Between the two world wars, Berlin developed into a fast-moving, cosmopolitan city. There were more than four million inhabitants and there was really a lot to see. Music halls sprung up, car races were held on the city's own track, the AVUS in the centre of town. The world's first television programme was broadcast at the 1935 Radio Exhibition. The KaDeWe was one of the biggest department stores in Europe and the Kurfürstendamm one of the continent's longest and most splendid boulevards.

Dark years

However, when world famous scientists like Albert Einstein started leaving Berlin and did not return from abroad, the people could feel that something was happening in the city that was really not so much fun. Even the Olympic Games that were held in Berlin in 1936 could not cover this up. Adolf Hitler and the National Socialists had come to power in 1933. They planned the eradication of the Jewish population and, in their delusions of grandeur, dreamed of creating a Pan-German Reich.

21

This Reich, with Berlin as its capital, was planned to stretch as far as Russia. The Nazi's war of extermination resulted in millions of deaths in Europe. Many cities – not only Berlin – were razed to the ground.

 You can find memorials to the 60,000 women who worked to clear away the rubble on Hasenheide and in front of the Red Town Hall.

A rude awakening

After the war and the liberation by the victorious Allies, Berlin looked like a gigantic rubble field. There were 600,000 destroyed apartments and only 2.8 million people still lived in the city. Many men had been killed in the war and it was the women who had to clear away the debris in the years after 1945 and take over the reconstruction work. Without these women, who worked night and day in the remains of the city, Berlin would have remained an enormous ruin for much longer.

A country is divided

The Allies, who had won the war, divided the former German Reich into occupation zones. Four years after the war had ended, there were two German states: the German Democratic Republic (the GDR) and the Federal Republic of Germany (the FRG). And Berlin was also divided into two sectors. While the two German states were struggling to establish themselves, the former Allies continued their determined fight for influence and power in the so-called "Cold War".

Raisin bombers

This led to the Soviet Union's blockade of West Berlin in 1948. West Berlin lay like an island in the middle of the GDR and was cut off from receiving any supplies by land. The western occupying powers – the USA, United Kingdom and France

– decided to set up an airlift to provide aid to the city.   Planes landed at Tempelhof airport every five minutes and brought the West Berliners food, soap and blankets. An American pilot came up with the idea of hanging sweets on miniature parachutes he had made himself and throwing them out of the cockpit window just before he landed. Soon other pilots followed his example. The planes were then nicknamed "raisin bombers" and the children ran to the Tempelhof airfield to try to catch the chewing gum and chocolate that came tumbling down out of the sky.

The Wall

After 1961, an almost four-metre-high wall was built that cut Berlin into two sections. It soon became impossible for the East Berliners to visit their friends and relatives living in the west part of the city. And, vice versa, it also became very difficult for the West Berliners to get into the east. The notorious Berlin Wall divided the city for almost 30 years. (You can find out more about the Wall and how people fled from East Berlin in R 1, R 2 and R 3.)

A big, united city

The wounds left by the war only started to heal slowly with the fall of the Berlin Wall in 1989 and the reunification of Germany in 1990. Today, Berlin has once again become a cheerful, lively city. The Berliners like to pack their bathing suits and spend their time swimming in Wannsee or Müggelsee.

Berlin has its own carnival and – since the exuberant fan mile at the World Football Championship in 2006 – people around the world have become acquainted with the spirit and humour of the Berliners. Jewish and French lifestyles have now returned to the city. You should not miss out on visiting the beautiful synagogue on Oranienburg Straße. And, if you would like to dance around or make music at one of the many new, colourful festivals, just come along to the street-music festival, the Fête de la Musique, that is held in the early summer in Berlin. Then you will be able to see with your own eyes – and feel in your legs as you dance around – just how cheerful things are in Berlin today.

1. Totatoes, Chocolate and Submarines

From Gendarmenmarkt to Checkpoint Charlie

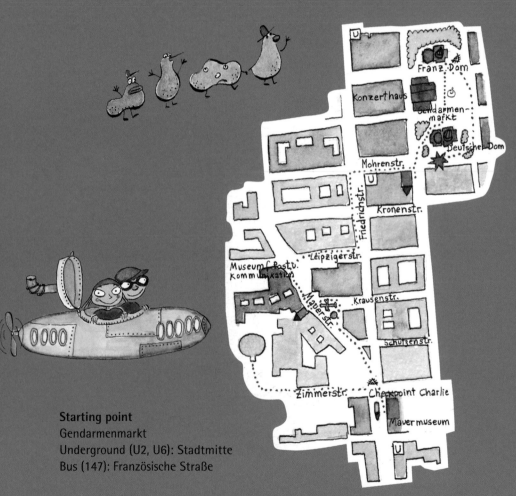

Starting point
Gendarmenmarkt
Underground (U2, U6): Stadtmitte
Bus (147): Französische Straße

The most beautiful square in Berlin
is located in the "Mitte" district and is
called the Gendarmenmarkt (Gendarme's
Market). At least the Berliners say that
and, until somebody finds a square that
is more beautiful, they are probably
right.

The first totatoes in Berlin
were sold here a long time
ago. In those days, the
German word for potato
"Kartoffel" was spelled
with a "t" instead of a "k".
Names change over time and the old
vegetable market where the totatoes
used to be sold is no longer called
Lindenmarkt but has been renamed
Gendarmenmarkt.

You won't find any watchmen
on Gendarmenmarkt but you will see
a lot of tourists, horse-drawn cabs and
bicycle rickshaws
called velotaxis.

You only have to take a few steps
from the underground station to see a
gigantic, colourful bear with its arms
raised high in the air. You won't need
a velotaxi for that. There are many of
these colourful giant bears in Berlin.
But you can easily see that the bear on
Gendarmenmarkt is different from all
the others: He has a funny giraffe on his
backside.

The German and French Cathedrals
next to the Concert House look like
mirror images of each other or twins.
Friedrich the Great, who the Berliners
liked to call "Old Fritz", had the domed
buildings built because he thought
that twin churches were beautiful.
But there are a few differences
between the cathedrals. If you come
to Gendarmenmarkt at noon, or 3 or 5
o'clock in the afternoon, you will even
be able to hear one of them. That's when
a glockenspiel with 60 different bells can
be heard (only) in the French
Cathedral.

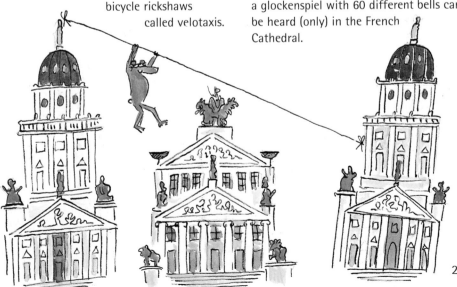

Religious freedom

Try to find the figure of a man wearing a turban at the entrance to the French Cathedral. He is a symbol for the religious freedom that Old Fritz granted to everybody in the 18th century. It made no difference to him if somebody was a Catholic, Lutheran, member of the Reformed Church, Jew or Moslem. His motto was: "Everybody should be happy in his own way."

before the French Huguenots arrived in their city. Potatoes were another new vegetable on the scene and we really have to ask ourselves what the Berliners actually ate up to that time.

"Ratzekahl" changes

That is why the Huguenots, religious refugees from France, came so eagerly to Berlin. Their history is shown in the Huguenot Museum in the French Cathedral. The French word "radical" was changed a bit and became "ratzekahl" in the Berlin dialect. Life in Berlin underwent a "ratzekahl" change with the arrival of the Huguenots. Old Fritz thanked them for this with a plaque on the outside of the cathedral.

Berlin gourmets

Old Fritz was especially amazed at the way the Huguenots managed to grow tobacco, artichokes and green peas on the poor sandy soil in Brandenburg. The Berliners had also never seen cauliflower, black salsify, asparagus and peaches

Speaking of potatoes

Potatoes once again played an important role on Gendarmenmarkt. In the 19th century, this was the site of the "Potato Revolution". This doesn't mean that the Berliners pelted each other with potatoes but that their hunger, as a result of the bad harvest, forced them to take to the streets and protest.

Concerts and festivals

not only take place in the Concert House today but also outside on the big square. Gendarmenmarkt is very pretty in the evening in the glow of the old lanterns. But, strangely enough, they

are also on during the day. Probably to make the square shine all the time.

On the roof of the big Concert House

you will see two griffons pulling a chariot with the Greek god Apollo inside it. The architect and painter Schinkel loved the theatre. That is why he had figures from the world of mythology attached all over the façade. However, he placed the two griffons with their beaks wide open and paws stretched forwards way up high on the ridge of the roof so that they would not frighten the Berliners too much. From close up, or with binoculars, you will see that they are really quite spine-chilling.

 A griffon is a mythical figure and a mixture of two animals. This is often a creature with a lion's body and an eagle's wings and head. Put together your own mythical figure or griffon from these animals.

In addition to a panther, you will find a lot of lions' heads on Gendarmenmarkt. Unfortunately, these lions had to work hard from morning to night. Anyone applying for this kind of work needed an extremely good set of teeth. That is because all of the lions' heads you find here have heavy, thick metal chains in their jaws.

 How many lions' heads can you find in front of the Concert House?

Chocolate dreams

Behind the German Cathedral, you can see Fassbender & Rausch, the biggest chocolate company in the world. The chocolate maker Fassbender used to deliver his wares to the royal court and the crowned heads and their families were almost driven out of their minds by his wonderful nougat and chocolate creations.

 This is probably a hungry customer who nibbled on the nose of the figure above the entrance door. Can you see it?

Sweet buildings

You will see the Brandenburg Gate, the German Parliament – the Reichstag – and the Memorial Church later on some other tours. But you can already get a close-up look at these Berlin buildings in the chocolate house. Here, however, they are made entirely out of chocolate but, unfortunately, you are not allowed to touch them or have a bite. You can also not nibble on the bubbling chocolate

volcano and giant bear.
But you can have a bite in the chocolate restaurant upstairs.

Friendly robots

You can recognize the Museum for Communication from far away by the three men struggling with a gigantic globe on its roof. Beneath this, in the atrium, you will be greeted by the house's three cheerful robots that look like gigantic kitchen scales or huge vacuum cleaners. They have funny names such as "Komm rein" (come in) and "Also gut" (ok, then).

 One of these robots is very friendly and likes to greet the visitors personally. Try to find out which one it is.

Dark cave

In the basement of the Museum, you go along a corridor and enter into a dark world of caves. If you stop in front of one of the columns there, you can find out why Germany's cheapest swimming pool only cost six kreuzers or admire the Blue Mauritius stamp – one of the most valuable in the world. And, if you are not yet fifteen years old, all of this fun won't cost you a cent.

A famous street

Many famous people, including Clemens Brentano, Heinrich von Kleist and Heinrich Heine, used to live on Mauerstraße. Today, most of the visitors to Berlin prefer gathering on the pavement and in the shops on neighbouring Friedrichstraße. This means that you can take a leisurely stroll along peaceful, pretty Mauerstraße with its renovated old houses on the right side.

A huge round package

If there was a lost-and-found office for giants, that is where the big, tied-up sphere that can be found on Mauerstraße would have been handed in long ago. Colourful chairs, ladders and other household items are tied together in this round package. This artistic ball is called the *Houseball* and is meant to show some of the things that refugees would take with them, or had to leave behind, when they were forced to flee from their country. It recalls the suffering of those émigrés who were driven out of their homeland of Bohemia in 1737 because of their religion.

 Can you imagine why the artist Claes Oldenburg also tied a cloud into this package?

 Find out which of the objects shown here are not on the ball.

Church labyrinth

Right next to the giant ball, you can see the outline of the old Bohemian Bethlehem Church on the ground. If you want, you can balance your way along the outline – or even skip along it. On the other side of the street at number 77 you can see a house where a craftsman had his workshop for a long time. A shield shows the work he used to do.

 What do you think was his trade?

up guards reminds us of this notorious border crossing. But you needn't be afraid; today's border guards are really friendly. You can get old visas (they are stamps that let you enter a country) and GDR stamps from them.

 Which one of these stamps would you like to have in your passport? If you don't like either of them, you can design your own.

Attention: the past

Just a few paving stones further on and you arrive at Checkpoint Charlie. A checkpoint is a place where people and their documents are checked and Charlie is the most famous one in all of Berlin. Today, the reconstruction of a border post with sandbags and dressed-

The Iron Curtain

Germany was already a divided country in 1961. But nobody in the East or West thought about a wall. The head of state of the GDR Walter Ulbricht had also promised that a wall would not be built. But it seems like there were simply too many people who wanted to escape from the East to the free West.

Dangerous dead end

And that is why West Berlin was walled in. Even busy Friedrichstraße was turned into a dangerous dead end for the people when a 3.6 metre high wall was erected there. Shortly after the wall had been built, American and Russian tanks armed with live ammunition faced each other at Checkpoint Charlie. They were only 200 metres apart. The entire world held its breath because everybody feared a Third World War.

Hot-air balloons and submarines

Of course, many East Germans wanted to live in the free West and came up with a lot of smart ideas about how they could escape. In their desperation, some of them dug tunnels, others built miniature submarines or kite-gliders. In the Wall Museum, you can see how somebody converted a small car, a Trabant, into an escape vehicle.

On your way out, try to discover where Georg Ehret hid his girlfriend in his car.

If you want to see Berlin from above, you can get into a hot-air balloon on Zimmerstraße. There is also still a small piece of the original Berlin Wall on this street.

Have we made it already?

2. Horses, Pigeons and a Pregnant Oyster

From the Brandenburg Gate to the House of World Cultures

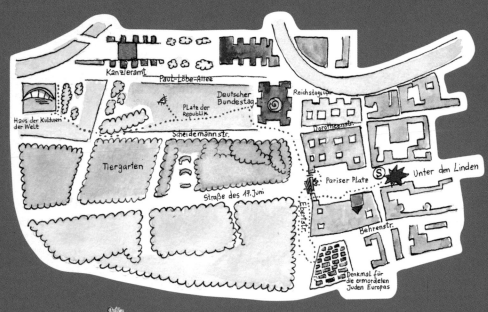

Starting point
Unter den Linden
Suburban train (S 1, S 2, S 25): Unter den Linden
Bus (TXL, 100): Suburban train station Unter den Linden

A narrow riding path

is all that the magnificent avenue Unter den Linden once was. In the 16th century, the prince electors rode along it on their magnificent horses from the City Castle to go hunting in the animal reserve. The horses you see here today draw coaches across Pariser Platz. Unfortunately, the beautiful sand riding paths no longer exist. There is only hard asphalt, which is not at all good for the horses' hoofs.

From the Hotel Adlon

you can see some horses that have no trouble at all with the asphalt because they don't even have to trot along the street. Maybe you have already discovered them on top of the Brandenburg Gate. But take a closer look around the reception area of the famous hotel. Charlie Chaplin, Marlene Dietrich and a few real maharajas have made their way across the red carpet. Here, you might also feel like pretending you are a star.

Four snorting horses

There can be no doubt that the beautiful chariot with the team of horses is one reason that the Brandenburg Gate has become Berlin's most famous landmark and a national symbol for all Germans. But, some others also took quite a liking to the famous Quadriga with the four horses. Napoleon had the entire ensemble dismantled and moved to Paris. However, when the French Emperor was defeated at Waterloo, the Quadriga came back to Berlin. The goddess of peace was turned into "Victoria", the goddess of victory and, since then, the Berliners have called the square in front of the Gate Pariser Platz.

HOTEL ADLON

33

If you stand underneath the Quadriga and look up, you will see one of the animals always looking you straight in the eye. But you will have to move around a bit. However, this trick does not work with one of the four horses. Which one could it be?

Into the time machine with you

You are now right in the heart of Berlin. But if you could get into a time machine that would take you back to the year 1740, you would find yourself standing on the edge of the city. In those days, the Brandenburg Gate was just one of many completely normal city gates and anybody wanting to enter Berlin here had to present their papers and – if they were a merchant – pay taxes. Today, you can come and go as often as you want – and you won't have to pay a cent.

Iron Gustav

Of course, such an important gate has been the setting for a lot of pleasant – and some not so pleasant – stories. One of the nicest is about the coachman who became famous as Iron Gustav. Because there were more and more cars in Berlin in 1928, and fewer and fewer people wanted to be driven in horse-drawn carriages, Gustav Hartman got into his hackney cab and – as a protest – drove to Paris with his team of horses.

The journey took him more than two months and the tough coachman was greeted with cheers when he reached the Eiffel Tower. He had already become a legend in Berlin because a clever newspaperman had reported on this adventure and the Berliners were well informed when Gustav finally made it back home. Tens of thousands of Berliners joined in the celebrations held under the Brandenburg Gate to honour his return. The writer Hans Fallada told the story of Iron Gustav and, of course, a film was also made of it.

But a few things were not mentioned in the film or the book: Iron Gustav owned a car and even had a license to drive a taxi!

Be careful, don't look now!

The goddess of victory driving the four horses on the Brandenburg Gate was originally completely naked – just the way the sculptor Schadow created her. But the drivers found it hard to concentrate on what they were doing and there were more and more rear-end collisions so that the decision was made to give the lady a little copper dress. As soon as that happened, the traffic started flowing freely again.

The field of steles

When you visit Berlin, going through the Brandenburg Gate a few times is supposed to bring you luck. And that is a good reason to go back there again soon. But before you do, you should visit the Holocaust Memorial. This is the largest monument in Berlin and is very important.

Like a swaying field of cornflowers

is the way the architect Peter Eisenmann imagined the 2711 concrete steles would look. They are intended to recall one of the most terrible crimes in German history – the murder of more than six million Jews in the period of National Socialism between 1933 and 1945. You just might lose your balance when you are making your way along the narrow paths because the ground is very uneven. But that is how it is meant to be because thinking about the horror of that period can easily make you dizzy.

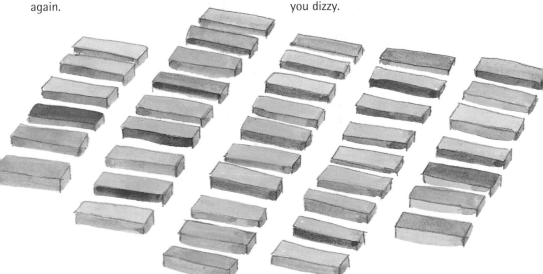

On the wall, on the wall ...
That is where the people leaped around and danced on the night between the 9th and 10th of November 1989 – the day when people say that the Berlin Wall fell. But it actually did not just topple then but remained standing for a while so that people could dance on it in their joy. The dancing was especially wild on the part of the wall right next to the Brandenburg Gate and the German Parliament, the Reichstag.

 Crossword puzzle
1. First name of a famous Berlin carriage driver?
2. What is the name for the team of four horses on the Brandenburg Gate?
3. *What is the name of the German parliament?*

4. *The House of Cultures has a curved roof that reminds one of this marine animal.*
5. *Which French emperor took the Quadriga to Paris?*
6. *What was Old Fritz' real first name?*
7. *Comfortable bikes that can take you around Berlin.*
8. *The surname of the British comedian Charlie who once stayed in the Hotel Adlon.*
Vertical red column: The name of the goddess of victory.

The Parliament – the Reichstag
The treaty between the four Allies said that Berlin could not be the capital city of Germany as long as the country was divided and the old government building – the Reichstag – went into a state of deep hibernation during those years.

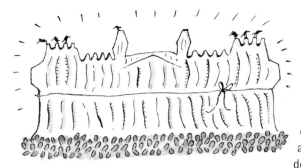

look up at the circular sky and ask themselves why the roof is not closed. But the members of parliament sitting in the plenary assembly hall are really happy to get the fresh air that is drawn down into the parliament and also the light that is reflected downwards by 360 mirrors. The architect had a real brainwave with this mirror-ventilation funnel.

But that all changed with the reunification. Once again great celebrations were held in the government district. The artist couple Christo and Jeanne-Claude threw an enormous white cloth over the Reichstag building. From a distance it looked just like a gigantic iceberg – in the centre of Berlin!

Magic mirrors

Norman Foster, the architect who renovated the Reichstag building, had a great sense of humour. He had the mirrors in the lifts that take visitors up to the observation platform made slightly curved. If you are too small, ask somebody to hold you up so that you can see the thousand people who fit into a single lift. The effect is caused by the mirrors reflecting each other.

The glass dome

But, the most fun is to wander up the ramp into the glass dome and stretch out on one of the benches at the top. Even adults like to lie down here and

Even the pigeons

think that the new Reichstag dome is a great idea. While the visitors look down on Berlin from on high and are happy to see how green the city is, the pigeons nest peacefully in the hall of mirrors and let their feathers flutter down.

Children's parliament

On special days, children from six to fourteen can try out what it is like to make politics in the Bundestag – the lower house of the parliament. This goes along with a tour of the building, the glass dome and finishes with a snack.

Children under the age of seven can get into the Reichstag building more quickly through a side entrance and can even take their parents and relatives with them.

Taking a velotaxi

is a really comfortable way to get to the House of World Cultures. Velotaxis are not expensive, but you can also walk; your route takes you through the beautiful Tiergarten and – depending on how long your legs are – you will only need ten to fifteen minutes.

The Chancellor's Office that you will see on your way is really new and already has a nickname – it is called the washing machine. Can you see the drum?

The pregnant oyster

The Berliners are famous for their cheeky tongues and like to give buildings clever, funny names. They call the House of World Cultures the "pregnant oyster" because its curved roof looks like an open oyster. The house used to be a congress hall but now it is an international culture house with a docking place for ships. It is close to the River Spree and water concerts are also held there. This is a fine place to dangle your feet in the water, listen to music, and sip a milkshake.

 Join the numbers and you will see an inviting oyster.

A giant butterfly

The German word for butterfly, "Schmetterling", sounds a bit severe; just not right for such a delicate animal with its gossamer wings. Maybe that is why the British artist Henry Moore called his ten-ton sculpture in front of the

House of Cultures of the World the "Giant Butterfly". If you look closely, you can see that – in spite of its massive dimensions – this work of art appears to be floating above the reflecting pool. Of course, Schmetterling does not come from the German word for "to break" (schmettern). It is related to the word for cream that is common in the east of the country and people used to say that butterflies liked to steal cream. So, you can see there is a connection to the English word "butterfly".

3. The Egyptian Queen and the Iron Monster

Around the Museum Island

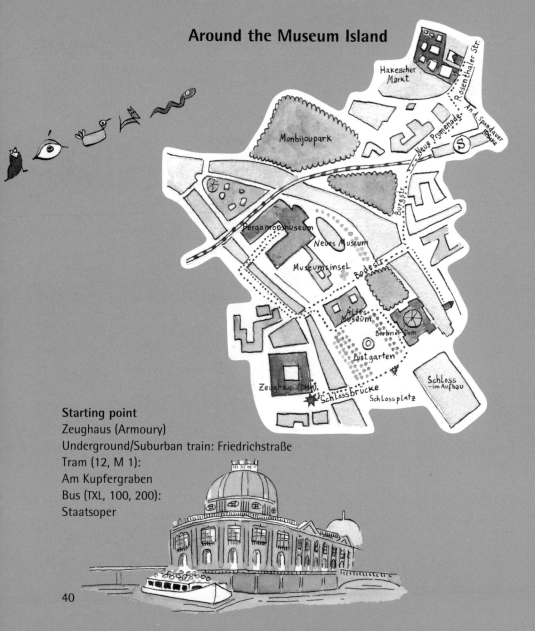

Starting point
Zeughaus (Armoury)
Underground/Suburban train: Friedrichstraße
Tram (12, M 1):
Am Kupfergraben
Bus (TXL, 100, 200):
Staatsoper

Cave chairs

When you stand in front of the gigantic armoury (Zeughaus) on Unter den Linden Boulevard, you will probably not be able to decide where to look first. The best thing to do is go in through the café entrance at Unter den Linden 2. There you can still see some funny hollowed-out chairs before you go through the big door and enter directly into the GHM, the German Historical Museum. You will soon find out what the GHM is – but what about these strange chairs? You could call them cave chairs because they arch over you in such a way that you feel that you could almost hide in one if you were small enough.

This child does not really want to sit in the air. Draw a cave chair around her.

Find the right key

There used to be a key game in the GHM. It was right next to the big mosaic on the first floor. It has to be repaired from time to time because the locks are very delicate. Ask if this fine game has been set up again.

 Which key fits this lock?

Huff and puff

Of course you can look at all of the knights' armour, magnificent helmets and victory trophies in the Museum. Have you ever tried to lift up a coat of chain mail? Here you can touch the knights' protective clothing and you will be surprised at how heavy it is – but don't get out of breath! You will still need a bit of stamina because the famous iron monster is waiting for you at the end of the tour – and you surely don't want to miss him.

Rattle!

Over the Castle Bridge

Take a close look at the railing of the

Castle Bridge. This is the only place in Berlin where you can see this mythical beast. Half horse and half fish. And its wings are wedged under its stomach. Most unusual! The fish that have been jammed in alongside this beast also don't seem to be too happy with their bent mouths. They had probably just been fished out of the water when the artist cast them in metal.

Want some potatoes?

The Lustgarten (Pleasure Garden) began its career as a garden with fruit trees, vegetables and flowers. Later, this is where the first potatoes were planted in Berlin. Remember them: the totatoes! Then it was transformed; fountains and statues were added, as well as a pleasure pavilion with an artificial grotto and

wonderful waterworks. The Berliners had a lot of fun in this pleasure garden until the Soldier King had everything torn down and turned into a parade ground. Luckily for us, the pleasure garden is green again today.

Giant bathtub

Today, a gigantic round bathtub made of granite has taken the place of the old canals and fountains in the pleasure garden. It was chiselled out of an enormous boulder in 1831. In summer, children turn it into a miniature swimming pool.

Stadtschloss (City Castle)

Of course, Berlin has a real castle. It was the main residence of the prince electors and, later, of the kings and emperors. It was severely damaged in the Second World War and blown up in the GDR era.

The Palace of the Republic stood on the site of the castle for thirty years. The City Castle is now being reconstructed opposite the Berlin Cathedral. Or, at least, one day we will be able to admire its façade again. It is planned that this will be the new home of the Humboldt Forum. This place of art, culture and science is named after the two scientist brothers Wilhelm and Alexander von Humboldt.

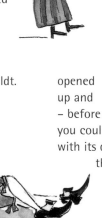

The magic table

In the 18th century, a prince elector had a very modern and practical apparatus installed in the castle. When the cooks in the cellar had set the table elegantly and it was overflowing with turkeys, trout, delicious sausages and wine, a servant set a lift into action. The decked table was put on a platform and raised into the dining room using a series of pulleys and hoists. A slab in the floor opened up and – before you could say one-two-three – the table with its delicious food stood in front of the prince elector. It sounds like a fairy tale but it is true and the Brothers Grimm based one of their stories on it.

Tomb or angels

Of course, you can climb up the 270 steps in the enormous Berlin Cathedral and look at the angels up there and down on the city. (It gets very narrow near the top and that is not always much fun for grown-ups.) But you can also go down to the tombs and see the magnificent sarcophaguses of Queen Sophie Charlotte and other members of the Hohenzollern family. This is a bit creepy and definitely not for scaredy-cats.

Beauty queen

The Berliners once voted to see who was the most beautiful woman in town – and chose a certain Nefertiti. If you don't know her already, you can find her in the Alte Museum. An Egyptologist called Borchardt found the bust many years ago near the pyramids in Cairo. She was the wife of the Egyptian Pharaoh Ikhnaton and, after his death, ruled one of the most powerful kingdoms of the time. Today, the bust of Nefertiti is one of the most valuable treasures in any of the world's museums.

Paint me, sweety!

 You will be able to see Nefertiti in the New Museum on the Museum Island when construction is completed.

The Museum Island

is a peninsula and, as the name tells you, packed full of museums. You would need weeks to see all the paintings, statues, jewels and costumes. But there is one museum you should not miss.

Pergamon and Babylon

You will feel like you are back in ancient times on the steps of the Pergamon Altar. A gigantic flight of stairs, columns and friezes showing the giants fighting against the Greek gods. The Ishtar Altar used to be one of the seven wonders of the ancient world. You will recognize dragons, along with lions and bulls, on its glazed bricks.

Which dragon would you chose to put on a city gate?

Nostalgia for the East

If you have not had enough of museums, you could make a detour and visit the GDR Museum that is on the mainland. It is great fun to take a ride in a rattling and clattering old Trabi car on its simulated trip through a prefabricated building settlement.

Colourful courtyards

Before you go on your way to the monsters, you should make a quick trip to the courtyards in the Hackesche Höfe. The entrance is at Rosenthalerstraße 38 and you can see its large round arch on the roof from far away. You will have no trouble finding your way out of the eight courtyards where people live, but grown-ups find this much more difficult and often get lost in Germany's largest enclosed courtyard area. There is a lot to see: cabarets, theatres, cinemas, cafés, arts and crafts shops, and beautiful façades decorated with colourfully glazed stones.

The iron monster

After all of those museums, you probably feel like seeing something really bizarre. There is an entrance to the right of the Hackesche Höfe. You can recognize it by the brass plate set into the ground pointing to the workshop for the blind from 1945. If you go all the way to the back of this colourfully painted courtyard, you will see an enormous monster bird. Unfortunately, the "monstermat" that you can use to make it move is usually broken. But, around the corner you will find another monster called the Bloch – and Bloch can do much more than just roll his eyes!

4. Knut, Knautschke and an Egg

From the Zoo Train Station to Breitscheidplatz

Starting point
Bahnhof Zoo (Zoo Train Station)
Underground/Suburban train: Zoologischer
Garten
Bus: 100, 110, 200 and many others
Local railway

The complete name

of the Zoo Train Station is really Berlin Zoological Garden. But, except for the conductors, no Berliner calls it that because it is just too long. While the city was still divided, it was the most important train station in the western section of the city. It became even more famous through the book and film "We Children from Bahnhof Zoo". It is the story of Christine F., a girl who was addicted to drugs, and led to many discussions about the children living on the Berlin streets.

A clear view

If you sit on the right side of the train passing the Zoo Train Station, you will be able to get a preview of the animal enclosures and see the giraffes eating.

The Lion Gate

is the entrance to the zoo with the greatest number of animal species in the world. The path to the right will take you to the elephants and pink flamingos. There is a petting zoo behind the monkey house where you can have close contact with the animals.

Cigarettes and coffee

Some animals have become real celebrities in Berlin. The first big stars in the 1920s were the female chimpanzees Titine and Missie; Missie was even allowed to smoke and drink coffee, something that it is strictly forbidden for the animals to do today.

Brave Knautschke

The only large animal that remained alive after the bombardment that rained down on Berlin in 1945 was a hippopotamus and the Berliners christened him Knautschke – from the German word for "crease or crumple" – because his face had looked so crumpled when he was born. Baby Knautschke survived the heavy shellfire between his dead parents and became a symbol for the Berliners to not hang their heads although the situation was desperate and get on with the work of rebuilding the destroyed city.

Hunger!

47

The bear christening

In times gone by, the boys and girls of Berlin were called on to think up original names for two little bears. Since then, it has been a tradition to hold a competition among the children of the city to name the Berlin bears and there is even a real bear christening. The famous bears Taps and Schnute are still famous today.

I don't care two hoots

The first panda bears were a real sensation and the Berliners called them Schnurz (couldn't care less) and Piepe (dead as a door nail) because they just sat around in their cage looking bored. At some stage, they were given the real Chinese names of Bao Bao and Tjen Tjen. But maybe it would have made more sense to stick to the popular Berlin names. The male bear Bao Bao just didn't care two hoots for the ladies. He behaved so badly when he visited a female panda in London that they could only be

separated by being hosed down with a fire extinguisher.

 Some of the animals in the zoo have been immortalized with sculptures. Try to find the granite sculpture of Bobby the gorilla!

A bear to smooch with

The little polar bear Knut was definitely the biggest star in recent times. When his mother refused to care for him, a foster father named Thomas Dörflein took on the task. Five hundred journalists travelled from all over the world when Knut was first presented to the public. Soon, everybody felt like smooching with Knut. But Knut was only really popular while he was small. Don't be disappointed if he is no longer in Berlin when you are there – he might have moved in with a pretty, shaggy girl bear somewhere else.

Things become really exciting with the sand tiger sharks, the giant snakes and the green moray eels – especially if you take a night-time tour. These are carried out by the light of pocket torches – and that can be pretty scary.

A giant dino

Of course, the Berliners always find new favourites among the animals such as Adolpho the anteater who really likes sticking his tongue out. But the zoo has not forgotten animals that became extinct a long time ago. You can see a life-size copy of the Iguanodon dinosaur next to the entrance to the aquarium. This is only a replica of a young animal – fully-grown, these dinosaurs were more than five metres tall, the same size as a giraffe.

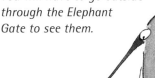 *After you have got to know the strawberry poison frogs, the Solomon Islands skink and octopus jellyfish, you will definitely be interested in the Stegosaurus and the Triceratops. Where can you find these animals? A hint: You will have to go outside through the Elephant Gate to see them.*

Kois and sharks

The animals are not quite as large and have better manners in the aquarium. There you can even stroke Japanese fish. They are really called koi carp.

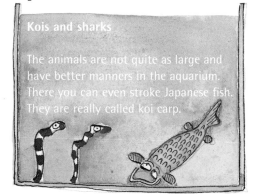

Water meatball

There is even more water in the Weltkugelbrunnen (Globe Fountain) that the Berliners simply call the "water meatball". What most people don't know is that work continues to be carried out on this fountain day and night. Can you find the metal worker with his welding goggles? And don't be afraid of what you find on your way. The grinning reptile on the edge of the pool is not a man-eating crocodile.

Time flows

The famous artist Salvador Dali liked to paint soft, melting clocks to show the phenomenon of time. But there are clocks that really flow, so-called water clocks. Unfortunately, they don't work very well outside in winter because they are much too slow when the water freezes and becomes ice. You can find a very beautiful water clock on the ground floor of the Europacenter. This water clock is called the "clock of flowing time" and stretches over three floors. If you want to see it, take the entrance opposite the big blue sphere. You will have to find out for yourself what is inside it because that changes. Over the years, it has been used as a discotheque and television studio.

A hollow tooth as a symbol

Breitscheidplatz, one of the most famous squares in Berlin, is known mainly for the Emperor Wilhelm Memorial Church. It was almost completely destroyed in a bombing raid in 1943. Today, you can only see the main tower (without its tapering roof) and the principal portal. The Berliners just call it the Memorial Church or "hollow tooth" because of the way it looks. Every hour, a glockenspiel plays to remind people of the horrors of war.

 Join the numbers and the Memorial Church will appear.

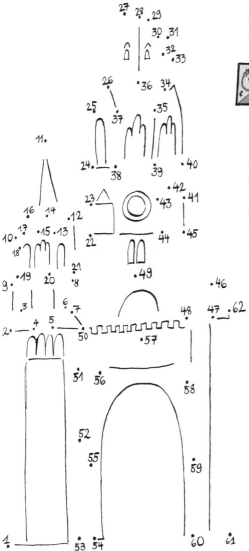

What happened to the egg?

The architect Egon Eiermann thought up a clever game of hide-and-seek in the new hexagonal nave – that the Berliners supposedly call the powder compact. In English, his family name means "egg man" and he hid an egg among the more than 40,000 coloured glass windows.

 You are not looking for a round egg but a rectangular one made of two letters. If you want to find it, take an especially close look at the windows near the pulpit.

Giant wheel

Soon you will be able to sit in a smart, white gondola and see the Memorial Church, the Zoo, the Tiergarten and much of the rest of Berlin from up on high. A 175-metre-high giant wheel is being built on Hertzallee near the zoo and it will be the biggest in Europe. For a long time, the Berliners discussed about whether the moving gondolas would disturb the animals in the zoo. But investigations showed that they couldn't care less. And so, soon not only people in Vienna and London will be able to see a wonderful panorama from a giant wheel – it will also be possible in Berlin.

5. The Lock and the Bats

From the Old City of Spandau to the Citadel

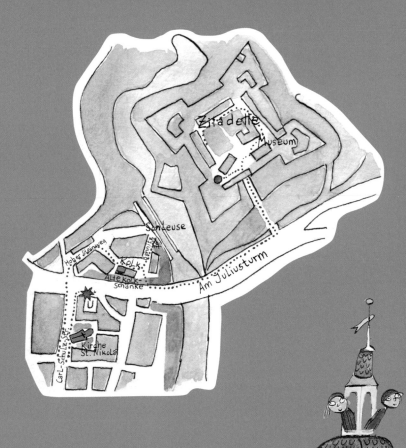

Starting point
Carl-Schurz-Straße
Underground (U 7): Altstadt Spandau

A short journey through time

An excursion to Spandau in the west of Berlin where the Spree flows into the Havel is a wonderful journey back in time. There are still cobblestone village streets and a massive castle citadel.

The town of Spandau

Today, Spandau is part of Berlin although some of the Spandauers don't want to admit that is really true. They say that they are first of all Spandauers and only then Berliners. That makes sense, because Spandau was an independent city until 1920. Today, it is only a half-hour underground ride from the centre of Berlin to the district on the Havel. In the Middle Ages, however, a courier on horseback needed almost half a day to get from Berlin-Cölln to Spandau.

Half-timbering

When you get out of the underground at Carl-Schurz-Straße in the old city of Spandau, you will find yourself in one of the biggest pedestrian precincts in Berlin. The half-timbered houses were all built in the years after 1740 because the older houses from the Middle Ages had been destroyed in a great fire. Only the old St. Nikolai Church remained intact. From the observation platform 54 metres up in the air you can see all the way to the citadel, Eiswerder Island and much, much further ...

Sparkling impressions

Some very mysterious activities started taking place on Eiswerder Island in 1829 and they soon became much louder. A laboratory was set up where fireworks were produced. Time and time again, people in the town could hear the bangs and explosions coming from the island when new fireworks were tried out. The Spandauers enjoyed the colourful racket: Unfortunately, the island was later used for making ammunition for wars and that was not so much fun.

Liebesinsel (Island of Love)

If you have good eyes, you will be able to see the Island of Love from the tower of St. Nikolai. The Berliners say it is called that because there are no bridges leading to the island. Today, lovers still like to take a boat over to the Island of Love where they can enjoy themselves without being disturbed.

Some crooked houses

Over time, the wood in half-timbered houses usually warps a little as you can see in the old inn "Alte Kolkschänke" that was built in 1743. The windows in the bar are particularly bent out of shape; it looks like they have become tired from their centuries of being windows and want to rest a little.

Danced crooked

But maybe the inn is crooked because so much dancing took place in it. In former times, people liked to dance in inns in the evening. There were regular police inspections because children were not supposed to be at these dances that lasted until late in the night. The mothers then hid their children under the wide skirts that were in fashion at the time.

Unspoiled old town

You can see what things used to look like in the village of Spandau if you take a stroll along the remains of the old city wall on Hoher Steinweg. This part of the old town used to be on an island. Next, turn to the right and go down the cobblestone street that is known as the Kolk.

Near the water

If you turn left at the end of the Kolk, you will see the Spandau Lock. Until the first lock was built in 1572, ships had to be pulled by oxen or horses because there was such a steep incline here. This new lock has been in operation since 2002. Now, even ships that are 110 metres long can pass from the Upper to the Lower Havel without any problems (and in the other direction too). Canoeists who think that it takes too long to raise and sink the water can carry their boats past along the side of the lock.

To reach the mighty citadel

you go across the Juliusturmbrücke. There are a lot of yachts and elegant sailing boats on the Havel and you can wave to them from up here. Before you go into the courtyard of the citadel, you should take a look at the different hats on the railings of a small bridge. One of them is what the Germans call a "Pickelhaube" – a helmet with a spike on top. Can you find this typical piece of Berlin headgear?

Over a drawbridge

and a wide moat, you make your way into the citadel. It is one of the best-preserved and most beautiful Renaissance fortresses in the world. And, it is one of the biggest. In the courtyard you can see some cannons, a few stone steps, and a snow-white statue of Margrave Albrecht the Bear.

 Two of the eight helmets are identical. Can you find out which ones they are?

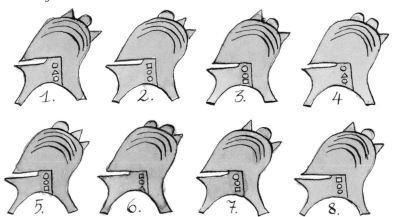

1. 2. 3. 4

5. 6. 7. 8.

55

The White Lady

One of the people imprisoned in the Julius Tower after 1572 was Anna Sydow, the lover of Prince Elector Joachim II. His son was supposed to take care of the lady after his father's death but he kept her locked up in the dungeon for the rest of her life. It is said that Anna turned herself into a ghost out of revenge and haunted the royal castles in Berlin as the White Lady for centuries.

Albrecht the Bear

from the house of Ascania was the founder of the Mark of Brandenburg and was often involved in battles. With the Saxons, for example, or against the robber barons. His age – the 12th century – was the time of knights and castles. It was easiest for the margrave to defend himself against the attacks of his marauding enemies in a castle built to resist a siege.

The tower prison

Today's citadel is the successor of this medieval castle. The fortress' location on the River Spree and its steep, high walls made it almost impossible for enemies to capture it. And, anybody taken prisoner was likely to end up in the dungeon behind the thick walls of the Julius Tower. Now you can climb up into this 30-metre-high tower over a steep, spiral staircase.

Medieval celebrations

In the citadel, children can take part in medieval cooking classes, learn how to bake bread on sticks and dine together like the knights of old. There is even a real shoemaker's workshop in the City History Museum and you will probably ask yourself just how the shoemaker could manage to work in such a mess.

Real vampires

Berlin is the bat capital of Germany. There are more than thirty places where the small, fluttering creatures can spend the winter in the city. Over 10,000 of them winter in the subterranean vaults, which are also known as casemates, of the citadel in Spandau. You can see how real vampires are fed at an exhibition cave in house number 4.

But you can also build your own bat nest or, for a small sum, become the honorary godparent of a leaf-nosed bat from the tropics.

Small guests

You cannot only find bats in Spandau but also in other districts such as Charlottenburg or Kreuzberg. Near parks, it sometimes happens that young, inexperienced animals flutter into flats through open windows and nest there. So, don't be surprised if you visit one of your friends in Berlin and find little vampires dangling from the ceiling.

6. The Lakeside Resort and the Alchemist

To the Pfaueninsel (Peacock Island) and Wannsee Beach

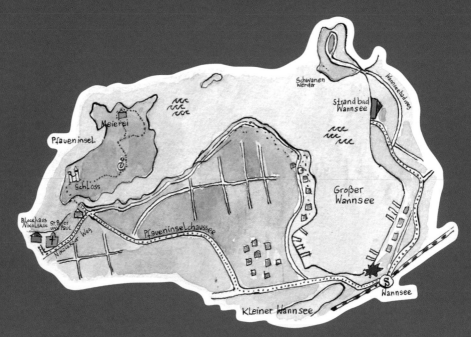

Starting point
Ferry to Pfaueninsel
Suburban train (S 1, S 7): Wannsee
Bus 218 (to Pfaueninsel ferry)
Bus 312 (from Suburban train
station Nikolasee to Wannsee
Beach)

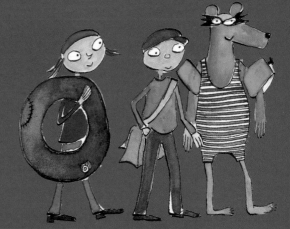

Into the open air

Of course you don't want to only walk on asphalt and cobblestones in a city that has more than 30 nature reserves and consists to one third of woods, parks, lakes and rivers. So, get out of the sea of houses and make your way to Wannsee!

Through wild Berlin

When you travel through the Grunewald (Green Forest) on the number 7 suburban train line, you will get an impression of just how huge it is. This used to be the prince electors' hunting grounds and today many wild animals still live in Berlin – not only in the zoo. The Grunewald is the home of foxes, martens, raccoons, wild boar and many other animals. Kestrels have moved into some town-hall towers in Berlin and beavers have even settled in along the River Havel and around the lakes that you can see to the left and right on your journey.

Ready for the island

Did you know that there are twice as many bridges in Berlin as in Venice? And there are more than enough rivers and lakes in the city.
And, of course, that means there are a lot of islands.

You can spend your holidays on 34 islands in Berlin. They have charming – and sometimes strange – names such as: Island of Youth, Pioneer Island, Island of Love or Water Nymph Wall. Now, we are going to visit one of the best-known and most beautiful of all the islands: Peacock Island.

 What does your dream island look like? And, what would you like to call it?

On the ferry

There is no bridge to Peacock Island but there is a ferry to take you across from the mainland. On your way over, you will see a little wooden shed on the right. This is where the small frigate "Royal Louise" is kept. Maybe the pretty, historical sailing ship will be anchored there when you visit.

A castle with a hut

If you go around the island to the left, you will see a white castle not far from the ferry station. There is an iron bridge between its two towers. King Friedrich Wilhelm II had it built for his lover Duchess Lichtenau. If you think the castle looks like it is in ruins, you are right – but it was meant to be like that. In those days, it was modern to pretend that something had broken out of the façade. On a tour, you will see that everything inside is just as it was in 1794. The "otehitic" cabinet is especially pretty. You will find a small room with a painted hut of palm trees and a lovely view – but it is also painted – hidden behind this strange name.

 The castle also has another painted view. Can you find out where it is?

Rabbit Island

For a long time, Peacock Island was known as Kaninchenwerder (Rabbit River Island) because rabbits were bred there after 1683. They multiplied rapidly and then hopped around all over the place.

The alchemist

Not long after the rabbits, the alchemist Johann Kunckel settled on the island where he wanted to produce gold. He wasn't very successful and most of the time stinking smoke drifted out of his chimney across to the mainland.

The first zoo

King Friedrich Wilhelm III, who owned Peacock Island at the beginning of the 19th century, had no time to waste on making gold, or alchemists and especially not on rabbits, but he was interested in exotic animals and peacocks. That is

why he created his own private zoo on Peacock Island with a pond for water birds, deer and water buffalo, a cage for kangaroos as well as llamas and – as you would expect from a "Bearliner" – a bear pit. The Berliners were allowed to come and have a peek at what the little llamas and kangaroos were up to on three days of the week.

Show-offs allowed

Today, the peacocks set the tone on the island. When it is warm, you can hear the call of the male birds from far away. Maybe you will be lucky enough to see one of the peacocks spread his colourful tail and you might even be able to get hold of one of the dazzling peacock feathers.

Fairy tale fountain

A path leads away from the castle on the right towards a big fountain with a round pool. On hot days, some visitors think of it as something out of a fairy tale. There is not a single restaurant on the island and a brief, refreshing cooling down in the enchanted peacock water is just what you need on a sticky summer's day. But, you shouldn't drink the water! Walk past the water-bird pond to the aviaries where the successors of the royal parrots and cockatoos used to flutter around. Today, there are no longer any exotic birds here and native species twitter away under the canopy of leaves.

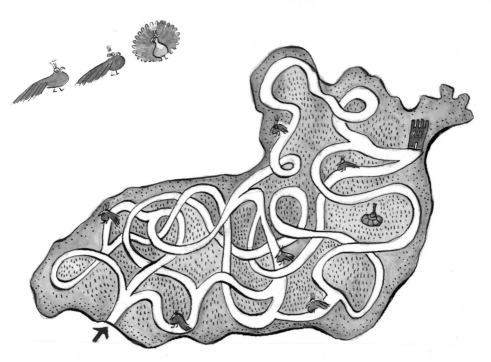

It is easy for people who are not careful to lose their way in a big park. Can you find the path leading to the ruin without coming across a bird?

On thin ice

Not only peacocks and other birds, but also horses and chickens have their home on the island. Sometimes in winter you can even see a fox or wild boar. They have simply come over the ice from the mainland.

A ruin or not?

You can find a dairy at the northern end of the island. Does it remind you of something else? Just like the castle, it was also built as a ruin. This time in the Gothic style. The dairy and castle look a little bit like film sets and films have actually been made on Peacock Island.

A little bit of Russia

Back on the mainland, you should first of all have a bite to eat in an inn. After that, you go to the right and find yourself in Russia. Or rather, a little bit of Russia in Grunewald.

The Nikolskoe log cabin is located on an observation platform that is easy to reach on foot. King Wilhelm III was received in a similar log cabin when he visited his daughter Princess Charlotte and her husband, the later Tsar Nicolas, in Russia. Charlotte said that it was possible to have as much fun in a simple log cabin as in an emperor's palace. The King liked it so much that he had this Russian-style log cabin built on Peacock Island. Later, the King added a Russian church with an onion tower; this is the Church of Saints Peter and Paul. From up here, you can get another fine view of Peacock Island.

Berlin's bathtub

Grab your swimsuit ... and don't forget your little sister ... and then off you go to Wannsee ... This is the beginning of

a German song that stormed the charts many years ago and no other lake in Berlin is as famous as Wannsee. One hundred years ago, the beach was one of the Berliners' most popular day-trip destinations and its 400 wicker beach chairs and 1200 sun beds were always chock-a-block in summer. The 31-metre-long giant slide is also a big hit. You will almost feel like you are at the seaside on the one kilometre long and 80 metre wide beach. And that comes as no surprise – the sand was brought here from the Baltic coast.

The water is especially shallow near the playground for small children.

7. Other Things to Do and See in and around Berlin

Now you know the inner city of Berlin, the mediaeval citadel and have taken a trip to Wannsee and Peacock Island. But, of course, there are so many other things to see and possibilities for exciting, amusing and interesting activities. To help you have a better overview, all of these suggestions have been grouped together:

Berlin panorama

A look at the universe and space travel

Palm trees, jungle, flowers

Berlin on the water

A short journey through time

Animals in the city

Magic tricks and juggling

Playing, letting off steam, riding

Films and film-making

Museums with special programmes for children

Emperor, king, nobility

Ship trips

Another square, another street

Berlin panorama

Television Tower

Alexanderplatz, Panoramastraße 1A
10178 Berlin, Underground/Suburban
train: Alexanderplatz
Info: 247 57 50
www.tv-turm.de

Its height of 368 metres makes the
Television Tower higher than all the other
towers in Germany. Fortunately, you don't
have to climb up a flight of stairs. Two
lifts whisk you all the way to the giant
observation sphere from where you can
see as far as the city limits more than 40
kilometres away – if the weather is fine.
For those who like to take things easily:
The Telecafé revolves around its own axis
in half an hour and you can watch Berlin
glide past you in comfort.

Victory Column (Siegessäule)

Straße des 17. Juni/Großer Stern
10557 Berlin, Suburban train: Bellevue,
Underground: Hansaplatz
Info: 391 29 61
www.monument-tales.de

People claim that no Berliner calls the
Television Tower the "Tele-asparagus".
But, the figure on top of the Victory
Column is really known as Golden Else.
You can climb up the 285 steps of
the spiral staircase to the top where
you have a wonderful view over the
Tiergarten.
A few bullet holes from the Second
World War can still be seen at the
bottom. The canon barrels that decorate
the column come from another war
against France.

Radio Tower

Masurenallee 14
14057 Berlin, Suburban train: Messe
Nord/ICC
Info: 303 83 900

The Radio Tower also has a nickname:
It is known as the "Langer Lulatsch"
which means something like "beanpole".
It could just as easily be called the
small Eiffel Tower because the two steel
constructions look very similar. The first
television programmes were transmitted
into the Berliners' living rooms from
this tower. Unbelievable but true: The
600 tons of steel rest on
porcelain. But you can
still go up; the porcelain
insulators are not as
delicate as teacups. They
can really take a lot!

A look at the universe and space travel

Zeiss-Großplanetarium

Prenzlauer Allee 80
10405 Berlin, Suburban train:
Prenzlauer Allee
Info: 421 84 50
www.sdtb.de
Two wonderful tours of the stars: The Little Star Dream or Stars, Fog, Fire Wheels. The stars are projected onto the dome for you. Fantastic space cinema!

Archenhold Observatory

Alt-Treptow 1
12435 Berlin, Suburban train: Treptower Park, Plänterwald
Info: 536 063 719
www.sdtb.de
Take a look through the longest refracting telescope in the world. You can even celebrate your birthday here or attend a lecture given by Mira the Star Fairy.

Planetarium

Wilhelm-Foerster-Sternwarte
Munsterdamm 90
12169 Berlin, Suburban train:
Priesterweg
Info: 790 09 30
www.wfs.be.schule.de
Astrology courses and the night of the dancing stars. And yes, the Big Bear really exists!

Orbitall in FEZ-Berlin

Straße zum FEZ 2
12459 Berlin, Suburban train: Wuhlheide
Info: 530 71-0
www.fez-berlin.de
Testing ground for young astronauts. Wobble discs and gym wheels are used to see if you are fit for space. Then, it's off to the space station – unfortunately, only a virtual one. But the earth really looks wonderful from above.

Palm trees, jungle, flowers

Botanical Gardens

Königin-Luise-Straße 6–8
14195 Berlin, Suburban train: Botanischer Garten
Info: 838 50 100
www.botanischer-garten-berlin.de
Do you want to watch plants grow? Seriously – there is a giant bamboo in the Botanical Gardens that shoots up 30 centimetres every day. And also: Get the feel of the jungle in the House of the Tropics and visit the special section where you are even allowed to touch the sweet-scented plants!

Potsdam Biosphere
*Georg-Hermann-
Allee 99
14469 Potsdam
Info: 0331–550 740
www.biosphaere-
potsdam.de*
There is even more jungle here with
real mangrove swamps, noises from
the primeval forest, and hot bubbling
geysers. There are stations where you
can carry out experiments; by turning a
crank you can watch a fern grow in fast
motion. Have a look at it!

Berlin on the water

Müggelsee
*Suburban train: Friedrichshagen
Strandbad: Fürstenwalder Damm 838
www.am-mueggelsee.de*
You can find Berlin's biggest lake
on the eastern border of the town.
Böldschestraße, with its small shops and
beautiful Jugendstil houses, leads from
the Friedrichshagen station
down to the lake. You then
turn to the left to reach the
Müggelsee Beach. You can also
walk to the 30-metre-high
Müggel Tower; after you
have climbed to the top, you
will have a fine view of the
lake. Those who are tired can
take the steamer back or
take another walk around
the lake.

Templin Beach
*Templiner Straße 102
14473 Potsdam
Info: 0331-661 98 37
Four kilometres along the bike path from
the Potsdam-Stadt station*
It is well worth the trip! Here, you won't
just lie around lazily in the sun: You
can visit a surfing school, learn how to
waterski, play table tennis or volleyball.
The beach with its shallow water is
especially suited for children.

Oberbaum Bridge
*Am Oberbaum
10997 Berlin
Underground: Warschauer Straße*
This bridge over the River Spree
used to be made of wood. Today,
the underground races by overhead
while you take a pleasant stroll down
below. There is no doubt that this is
the most beautiful bridge in Berlin and
the famous Oberbaum battle between
Kreuzberg and Friedrichshain takes place
here in summer. That is when the two
sides pelt each other with rotten fruit
and vegetables. The first one to leave the
bridge is the loser.

Fairy tale Fountain
In the Volkspark Friedrichshain
Entrance: Am Friedrichshain and
Friedenstraße
www.berlin-friedrichshain.com/
volkspark.htm
This is the right fountain for you if you
want to kiss a frog. Here, nine frogs
spout water into the terraced pool.
There are other figures from the fairy
tales of the Brothers Grimm around the
edge of the pool – from Hans in Luck,
Cinderella and Little Red Riding
Hood to Little Brother and Little
Sister.

AquaDom & Sea Life
Spandauer Straße 3
10178 Berlin, Suburban train:
Alexanderplatz, Hackescher Markt
Info: 992 800
www.sealifeeurope.com
This water theme park offers an
underwater tunnel, sunken ships and a
countless number of fish in more than
30 pools. The grand finale is a ride in a
lift through a gigantic aquarium with
sharks, sea horses and stingrays.

A short journey through time

Domäne Dahlem
Königin-Luise-Straße 49
14195 Berlin, Underground: Dahlem-Dorf
Info: 666 30 00
www.domaene-dahlem.de
The open-air museum in the former
manor of Dahlem shows you how pigs,
cows and sheep used to be kept in Berlin.
Goldsmiths, basket weavers and glass
blowers give demonstrations of their old
crafts at market festivals. You can drive
a tractor, feed the animals and make
things with beeswax.

Düppel Museum Village
Clauertstraße 11
14163 Berlin, Suburban train:
Mexikoplatz, Zehlendorf
Info: 802 66 71
www.dueppel.de
Here you can really immerse yourself
in the Middle Ages. You can cook food
in pot-bellied kettles, shear sheep, see
what the blacksmith is up to, discover
historical children's games like ring

spearing or hoop rolling, and eat flat bread. The people in the Düppel Museum village are even dressed like they were in the Middle Ages and that makes this journey back in time even more authentic.

Animals in the city

Animal Park Berlin-Friedrichsfelde
Am Tierpark 125
10319 Berlin, Underground: Tierpark
Info: 515 310
www.tierpark-berlin.de
You already know the zoo. The animals in Berlin-Friedrichsfelde have even more space because the park is not cramped in the centre of town. The spotted hyenas and baby elephants love that. And, there is even a real castle in the middle of the animal park.

Magic tricks and juggling

ufaFabrik Circus
Viktoriastraße 10-18
12105 Berlin,
Underground:
Ullsteinstraße
Info: 755 030
www.ufafabrik.de/circus
There is a flea-market for children, a puppet theatre, lantern festivals, children's concerts, a farm for children and much, much more in the ufaFabrik. Those who have dreamed of being a clown or acrobat can visit the circus school. Some of the monocycle artists, tumblers and jugglers who have made a career on Broadway in New York or in Japan started here. The circus has existed for more than 20 years. If acrobatics are too strenuous for you, you can have a try at samba drumming or oriental dancing.

Playing, letting off steam, riding

Staaken Pony Farm
Cosmarweg 70
13591 Berlin, Bus 131: Springerzeile
Info: 366 89 42
It is not only possible to ride horses or ponies; you can just as easily ride a donkey. If you don't believe so, this is where you can find out if it is true. And you can also see a goat, geese and sheep.

Telux Adventure Playground
Tegeler Straße 28a
13353 Berlin, Suburban train: Wedding,
Underground: Leopoldplatz
Info: 462 98 29
Here you can build huts, plant vegetables, have mud fights, make pottery, repair your bike and publish your own newspaper – and all of that to your heart's content. This adventure playground is a bit different from all the others!

Jungle Playground in Bäkepark
Dalandweg 34
12167 Berlin, Suburban train: Lankwitz
Climbing castles and hanging bridges. Climb hand over hand, swing and hop around under palm trees between wild panthers and giraffes.

Films and film-making

Filmpark Babelsberg
August-Bebelstraße 26–33
Entrance Großbeerenstraße
14482 Potsdam, Suburban train:
Babelsberg
Info: 0331–721 27 50
www.filmpark.de
Here, in the studios of the dream factory, painters, makeup artists and set designers show you what goes on behind the scenes of making a film. How many petticoats does a rococo costume have? What does it feel like to be in a submarine? Try it out! In Babelsberg, there are so many possibilities for this!

Museums with special programmes for children

Germany Museum of Technology Berlin
Trebbiner Straße 9
10963 Berlin, Suburban train: Anhalter
Bahnhof, Underground: Gleisdreieck
Info: 902 540
www.sdtb.de
This is one museum you really should not miss! You can recognize the museum from  far away by the big plane hanging on the outside under the roof. There is so much to see and the best place to start is in the Spectrum. Here, you will find out about all the things children are interested in. More than 300 experiments show you why the sky is blue or how a battery works. You will also discover all you need to know about navigation, windmills, television studios, rockets and solar power plants. And much, much more ...

Sugar-Museum
Amrumer Straße 32
13353 Berlin, Underground: Amrumer
Straße
Info: 314 275 74
www.sdtb.de
Even though your dentist warned you
about it, this is where all those with a
sweet tooth – and even those who don't
like sugary things – can find out all they
need to know. It is all about the history
of sugar production from sugar cane to
sugar beets and back again ...

JuniorMuseum in the Ethnological Museum
Arnimallee 23
14195 Berlin, Underground: Dahlem-Dorf
Info: 830 14 38
www.juniormuseum-berlin.de
This used to be called the Museum for
the Study of Human Races and it still
deals with the people of our world. Trips
through the Sahara to the Touareg, or
to the Aborigines in Australia,
show you how and why
you can write in the sand
or throw a boomerang.

A short journey around the world that is
really worth taking.

Museum of Natural History
Invalidenstraße 43
10115 Berlin, Underground: Zinnowitzer
Straße
Info: 209 385 91
www.museum.hu-berlin.de
Many other surprising things await
you after you have gotten over the
first shock of seeing some huge sharks'
jaws. The famous primeval bird, the
Archaeopteryx, for example. It is world-
famous and scientists from all around
the globe come here to admire it!
Do you like gruesome, giant dinosaur
skeletons? In the main hall of the
museum you can see just how big a
fully-grown Brachiosaurus or Dipodocus
could be. The Brachiosaurus is the largest
skeleton in the world, so take a deep
breath and get a good
look at it. You can
relax afterwards on
the beautiful round
sofa in the cosmos
and solar star hall.

Emperor, king, nobility

Charlottenburg Castle

Spandauer Damm 10–22, 20–24 14059 Berlin, Suburban train: Westend, Underground: Richard-Wagner-Platz
Info: 32 09 11

Charlottenburg has everything a real castle should have: Magnificent halls of mirrors, precious furniture and an enormous castle park. You don't have to put on any heavy velvet or stiff brocade clothes to go on a guided tour through the rooms where the kings and queens used to reside. But, the paintings show you that this is how people used to run around. The porcelain cabinet is especially precious. Old Fritz was a great admirer of what is called "white gold" and once bought the porcelain factory to have his own tableware produced. If you happen to drink your hot chocolate out of a cup with a royal blue sceptre on the bottom, you can be sure that it was made in the Royal Porcelain Factory (KPM) and is really worth a lot of money.

Sanssouci

Maulbeerallee, 14469 Potsdam, Suburban train: Potsdam Hauptbahnhof, Bus 695
Info: 0331–969 42 02
www.sanssouci-sightseeing.de

Potsdam is not actually a part of Berlin but it would really be a pity if you missed out on this charming castle. It is only a fifteen minute drive by car from Peacock Island. Friedrich the Great who built the castle had an extremely tough and strict childhood and was happy to be able to live – more or less – without cares when he was an adult. That is why he called his favourite castle Sanssouci – it is French for "free from cares"! Children can take part in special prince and princess tours on Mondays; at the end, they can play being artists. By the way, Old Fritz is buried in a crypt in Sanssouci alongside his favourite dogs. You can recognize this place by the potatoes that some visitors place there. Of course, you know already that Friedrich was the person who made totatoes

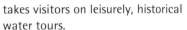

popular in Berlin. That is why some people are even fond of calling him Pommes Fritz.

Ship trips

Berliner Geschichtswerkstatt e.V.

Goltzstraße 49
10781 Berlin, Underground: Eisenacher Straße
Info: 215 44 50
www.berliner-geschichtswerkstatt.de
It might not sound terribly exciting, but it is. Children can take the ship "Käpt'n Cook" on a tour of the city's waterways. Young pirates will need a bit of patience though; the trips can take more than three hours. So, don't forget to bring along enough provisions!

Stern- und Kreisschifffahrt

Puschkinallee 16–17
12435 Berlin, various starting points
Info: 536 36 00
www.sternundkreis.de
In the Mouth of Moby Dick or the Havel Queen over the Landwehrkanal and River Spree. This is where you pass through the most locks – and that is always exciting. The steamer "Kaiser Friedrich" was built in 1886 and, today,

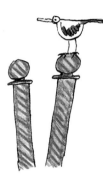

takes visitors on leisurely, historical water tours.

Bruno Winkler Shipping Company

Mierendorffstraße 16
10589 Berlin Charlottenburg
Info: 349 95 95
www.reedereiwinkler.de
If you want to have a fine meal while travelling on the waterways in the centre of Berlin, you can take part in the family brunch on the Spreekrone in summer. Children between 7 and 14 years of age only pay one euro for each year on this gourmet tour. At special times, there are leisurely cruises around the Müggel Hills and you can see the Wannsee ablaze during the big fireworks display on the water in September.

Riedel Shipping Company

Planufer 78
10967 Berlin, various starting points
Info: 616 579 30
www.reederei-riedel.de
If you don't feel like walking all the way around the Museum Island, you can have yourself taken around on the water. You will also see the charming Nikolai district. The atmospheric evening city tours are especially recommended for night owls and patient children.

Another sqare, another street

Potsdamer Platz
Suburban train: Potsdamer Platz
You can really get the feel of being in a big city on Potsdamer Platz, Berlin's most modern square. Here, architects have dreamt up absolutely crazy skyscrapers. Don't miss the tented roof of the Sony Center. This is where Berlin's heart beat in the 1920s and today it is still a major traffic junction. You can get a look at the first traffic light in Berlin and a section of the legendary Kaisersaal (Emperor's Hall); it is in a glass box next to the Sony Center.

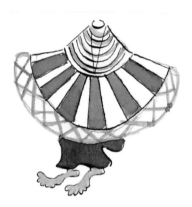

Kurfürstendamm
U-Bahn: Kurfürstendamm
Is there anybody who has not heard about the famous Kurfürstendamm? The Berliners simply call it Ku'damm. It started its career as a riding path (just like many of the other major avenues and boulevards in Berlin!). This was the path that took the prince electors directly from the City Castle to the Grunewald hunting estate. (You should have a look at that, too; it has the oldest castle in Berlin!) For a time, Kurfürstendamm was completely laid out with wooden beams and people called it Knüppeldamm (Cudgel Dam). After Chancellor Otto von Bismarck had seen the Avenue des Champs-Elysées with the Arch of Triumph in Paris, he decided that he absolutely had to have such a magnificent street in Berlin! And now, Kurfürstendamm is a 3.5 kilometre long shopping street. It used to be a symbol for the economic miracle of the 1950s. It has lost some of its importance since the reunification of Germany. But, nevertheless, it is still very famous!

Puzzle Answers

Page 27: You can find 27 lion heads in front of the Concert House – but they don't bite!

Page 28: The friendly robot is silver coloured and is called »Komm rein« (Come in!)

Page 29: The clouds in the Houseball symbolize freedom; something that is important for all people and especially for refugees.

Page 30: The person who lived in Mauerstraße 77 was a blacksmith.

Page 31: Georg Ehret hid his girlfriend under a black cloth on the front passenger seat when the two made their escape.

Page 34: The second horse from the right! It isn't looking down.

Page 36: 1. Gustav; 2. Quadriga; 3. Reichstag; 4. Oyster; 5. Napoleon; 6. Friedrich; 7. Velotaxi; 8. Chaplin. The name of the goddess of victory is Victoria.

Page 41: It is the third key.

Page 48: You can find the granite sculpture of Bobby the gorilla near the monkey house.

Page 49: You can find the Stegosaurus and Triceratops, along with other dinosaurs, outside to the right of the Elephant Gate on the façade of the aquarium.

Page 55: The identical helmets are number 3 and number 7.

Page 60: It is the view through the castle gate that was only painted. You can see a landscape with small trees and you can also make out a part of the portcullis in the upper section of the painting.

Index

Brigitta Höpler · Sibylle Vogel ·
Alexander Potyka

Vienna
City Guide for
Children

Translated by Robert Scott McInnes
80 Seiten, four-colour, Paperback
ISBN 978-3-85452-863-9

Shortlist for the Austrian Award
for Children's Books and Juvenile
Literature 2003
Federhasenpreis 2001

There is so much to see and discover in Vienna – you just have to know where
to look. This book, full of practical tips, entertaining puzzles and illustrations,
and many interesting facts, playfully guides children on six tours through the
city. The light-hearted expedition shows that a city sightseeing tour can be as
much fun for children as for grown-ups.

This City Guide for Children is also available in German
Wien – Stadtführer für Kinder,

by Brigitta Höpler, Sibylle Vogel, Alexander Potyka
ISBN 978-3-85452-856-2